an extract from

michel faber's

under the skin

with an enthusiast's view
by mary firth

an extract from
michel faber's
under the skin
with an enthusiast's view
by mary firth

Scottish **Book** Trust

2003

Published by
Scottish Book Trust
Scottish Book Centre
137 Dundee Street
Edinburgh EH11 1BG

Tel: 0131 229 3663

From April 2003 Scottish Book Trust will be moving its offices to Sandeman House, 55 High Street, Edinburgh EH1 1SR.

ISBN: 1 901077 03 9
Copyright © Scottish Book Trust, 2003

Published with the support of the Scottish Arts Council National Lottery Fund and The Hugh Fraser Foundation.

Under the Skin is published by Canongate
ISBN 1 84195 094 7

Extract copyright © Michel Faber, 2000

Series design by Caleb Rutherford eidetic
Printed in the UK by Cox & Wyman, Reading, Berkshire

contents

read **around books**

There is no shortage of fiction on the shelves of our bookshops – quite the opposite – but finding one that shouts out 'this is what you are looking for' is getting harder and harder as the number of books published goes up with each passing year. Too often we open a new book with expectation and enthusiasm only to discover disappointment and to struggle to get beyond page thirty. When we do find a book we really enjoy the urge is there to tell friends, colleagues and family to read it too in the hope that they will share our delight.

Read Around Books goes one step further and puts that enthusiasm down in black and white in the hope that many more readers will discover the joys of reading the very finest fiction that has emerged from Scotland over the last one hundred years. **This is a chance to sample before you borrow or buy**. Others have found these books before you, the writing held them spellbound and even when finished, these books would not let their readers go.

Each of the first twelve of these highly collectable little guide books promotes a work of fiction by a writer who lives in Scotland, was born in Scotland or who has been influenced by Scotland (our definition of Scottish is generous). Together they offer a marvellous introduction to the very best of Scottish writing from the twentieth and the first few years of the twenty-first centuries.

In each you will find a substantial extract, the enthusiast's view of the book, starting points for discussion for readers' groups, a short biographical piece about the author, and suggestions for similar reads which act as a further gateway to fine fiction.

Jan Rutherford
Series editor, 2003

the enthusiast

Mary Firth

Mary Firth is a graduate of Edinburgh University and is presently an English teacher at Hutchesons' Grammar School, Glasgow. She is the co-author of a number of textbooks on English language and literature which are used widely in senior schools both in Scotland and throughout the UK. The latest title, *Studying the Novel,* has just been published by Hodder Gibson.

the enthusiast's **view**

Under the Skin

by Mary Firth

'... the real triumph is Faber's restrained, almost opaque prose. This is a man who would give Conrad a run at writing the perfect sentence... Room will now have to be made for Faber alongside Alasdair Gray, James Kelman, Irvine Welsh and A.L. Kennedy.'
– *Guardian*

Michel Faber's work has been described as a cross between Roald Dahl and Franz Kafka. His first novel, *Under the Skin*, confirms that description, taking the reader on an extraordinary, utterly unexpected but equally compelling journey into a dark and disorientating world. It begins with a tease. Within a few pages, we feel as if we have been led into a maze. We proceed along some apparently well worn paths, but each time we think we know where we are going, a sudden twist reveals a completely unexpected direction in the plot.

Faber reveals the many facets of the lead character slowly and with great skill. At the start, we meet a young woman cruising along the A9 on the look-out for muscular male hitch-hikers – 'a hunk on legs'. We're told she has been doing this 'for years'. Is she then a rather foolhardy sister of Bridget Jones? Will she meet Mr Right standing by the road with a placard saying 'Inverness'? Her provocative behaviour with the first hitch-hiker leads us to feel she is more likely to end up dead in a ditch after giving a lift to Mr Wrong. Could we be in whodunnit, Ruth Rendell territory, then?

But this young woman doesn't seem like a victim; she has a most astonishingly predatory attitude to the opposite sex. As she admires her latest pick-up out of the corner of her eye, 'savouring the thought of how superb he'd be once he was naked', we are told she is already looking out for 'an even better prospect'. And by the end of chapter one we have learned that it is not she who is destined to be the victim: the first hitch-hiker has been drugged via an elaborate system of hypodermic needles built into the passenger seat of her car and is obviously the latest in a gruesome tally, as she bizarrely dresses him up in a wig and glasses so that he looks 'much like the others'. Ah, right. A female Hannibal Lecter, then. A mad psychopath, perhaps avenging herself on the male sex? No, not even warm.

This is a book that defies pegging by genre. It is strikingly original and imaginative. When we do finally find out what it is all about, we realise there have been clues there all along. There is the heroine's peculiar name, 'Isserley', for a start. She refers to the hitch-hikers as 'bipeds'. We are casually told the controls of her car include levers for lights, indicators, windscreen wipers and 'icpathua'. What on earth is 'icpathua'? Most telling of all there are the details which are revealed about her own appearance. The narrative switches neatly from her point of view to that of the various men she picks up, as they mentally evaluate her assets. She is unusually tiny, and oddly proportioned, with strangely deformed claw-like hands. She seems to smell, not unpleasantly, of seawater. Although she has a pretty little nose and 'a fantastic big-lipped supermodel mouth', she wears ultra-thick glasses which make her eyes look huge. The hitch-hikers are particularly fascinated by her large, perfect, Playboy-model breasts which emerge from a skimpy black top, worn despite the Scottish weather outside.

Gradually, the truth emerges. Isserley is a being from another planet who has had special plastic surgery to make her appearance conform to their – slightly inaccurate – idea of the female inhabitants of planet Earth. (The breasts, for example, were based on a photograph from a magazine). Isserley kidnaps human males ('vodsels' in her language), for a large and sinister organisation, Vess Industries. The 'vodsels', having been rendered unconscious by the 'icpathua' drug, have their tongues cut out. They are then castrated, fattened up in squalid dens and eventually slaughtered before being exported to this alien community for whom their flesh is the ultimate delicacy. This barbaric cruelty is played out against the stunning landscape of the Scottish Highlands.

At the isolated farm which is the headquarters of Vess Industries, there is a massive, subterranean multi-storey complex in which the victims are 'processed' by a team of workers, who retain their original shape – unlike Isserley they do not mix with the inhabitants of earth and so do not need to be modified. They go on all fours, have prehensile tails, and their bodies are covered in fur. They have prominent dog-like snouts and large eyes and ears. Isserley has had her tail amputated, her spine straightened and her front paws and facial features altered. She must regularly shave her face and body. Her eyes are disguised behind thick glasses to make their huge size look like the result of refraction.

The mere mention of aliens will doubtless send many readers who 'never read fantasy' or 'hate science fiction' scurrying for cover. However, those willing to suspend their prejudices will be rewarded.

Faber gives us a large spoonful of reality with which to swallow the fantasy. *Under the Skin* is a topographical novel, set largely on the remote coastal regions of Easter Ross, as well as on the A9 highway. With Isserley, we drive over the Dornoch Firth and the Kessock Bridge, from Tain to Inverness and back again, and out the little road to Portmahomack somewhere along which the sinister Ablach Farm (meaning 'place of slaughter') is situated. Does 'Donny's Garage' in the village of Kildary actually exist? I don't know, but Isserley's battered red Corolla becomes as real as the A9 itself.

Then there is the character of Isserley and her touching vulnerability. She is almost always in some sort of pain which intensifies as the story proceeds till she is at screaming point. Her constant driving, back and forth, back and forth, along the same lonely stretch of road has a nightmarish quality. Her body aches following her mutilating operations, she is frequently tired and dizzy with sleeplessness and faint from hunger, as she cannot tolerate 'vodsel' food. She wrestles with adverse driving conditions and is dazzled by oncoming headlights until she almost crashes.

The boorishness and patronising contempt with which most of the hitch-hikers treat her also channel our sympathies towards her. When Isserley is subjected to a brutal sexual assault, she kills her attacker by gouging his eyes with her steely strong fingers. However, it is the fact that she must return to this gory scene to retrieve a lost fingernail which might betray the presence of aliens to the authorities that most disturbs the reader.

Isserley's perpetual travelling turns into a journey of self discovery. At first she entraps her victims and calmly consigns them to their fate. To Isserley and her alien race, the inhabitants of earth seem a subhuman species. The arrival of Amlis Vess, the son of the head of Vess Industries, is a turning point for Isserley. Amlis has stowed away in one of the spaceships in order to investigate. He is horrified at what he discovers and one of his first acts is to release some of the captives. He desperately tries to open Isserley's eyes to the degrading cruelty involved.

One of the most stomach-churning sequences in the book (and yet highly intriguing for the reader) is when Amlis persuades Isserley to descend to the lowest level of the complex to view the prisoners in the 'vodsel pens'. Isserley finds them confined in near darkness, in 'a stench of fermenting urine and faeces'. One captive desperately scratches the word 'Mercy' in the dirt. Although Isserley claims not to understand this 'vodsel' word, Amlis quietly says he can guess its meaning. He awakens in her the disturbing realisation that she and the 'vodsels' may not be that different 'under the skin'. Despite being in apparent denial, Isserley forces herself to confront the horrors of the slaughterhouse itself. Here at last she becomes aware of exactly what she has been a part of and from this point on, the tragic outcome becomes inevitable. After Amlis is transported home in disgrace, Isserley is left isolated in an alien world where she has rejected her own kind.

Under The Skin is also a story of unrequited love. Isserley falls in love with Amlis Vess and it is Faber's achievement to present us with this alien being through her eyes so that we, too, can see him as a beautiful and charismatic figure, effortlessly superior in physique and mentality: 'Amlis Vess had a soft down of flawless black from the tips of his ears to the curve of his throat, as if lovingly tooled in black suede by an idealistic craftsman. Deeply set in this perfection of blackness, his tawny eyes shone like illuminated amber.'

Isserley suppresses her feelings for Amlis, as she is determined to despise him as a spoilt and privileged scion of the upper classes, and she resents his gentle courtesy as he awakens disquieting pangs of conscience within her. Although we are told Amlis finds her beautiful 'in her own way', she feels humiliated by what she sees as the disfiguring effects of the plastic surgery which has transformed her into the shape of a 'vodsel'.

Like Isserley, Amlis is moved by the natural wonders of the earth. The evening before Amlis is due to be deported, Isserley drives him to the sea where he is awe-struck by its beauty and immensity. The enchantment is complete when it begins to snow. During this shared experience they finally become close. Amlis shows her how to gain some respite from the excruciating pain she is suffering by chewing icpathua, the tranquilliser drug. But more importantly, he also guides her towards spiritual comfort, advising her to 'listen to the voice inside her'.

It is impossible to read this novel without becoming deeply involved. Faber toys with our perceptions; humans become 'animals', and aliens 'humans' in a wonderful parallel between the day-to-day of our own world and this explosion of imagination. He leads us to examine the human condition from outside, and produces a tale with many tantalising layers of meaning which will linger in the mind for a long time.

The extract

Under the Skin

chapter 4

It was as she was crossing a concrete tightrope, high up in the air, that Isserley admitted to herself that she absolutely did not want to meet Amlis Vess.

She was driving towards the midpoint of the Kessock Bridge, gripping the steering wheel in anticipation of fierce side-winds trying to sweep her little red car into space. She was acutely conscious of the weight of the cast-iron undercarriage beneath her, the purchase of the tyres on the bitumen – paradoxical reminders of solidity. The car might have been protesting how heavy and immovable it was, in its fear of being moved.

You-ou-ou-ou-ou-ou-ou! jeered the atmosphere.

At intervals along the bridge were trembling metal signs depicting a stylized net inflated by the thrust of a gale. This, like all traffic symbols, had been a meaningless hieroglyphic to Isserley when she'd first studied it, long ago. Now it appealed directly to her second nature, and made her seize hold of the wheel as if it were an animal desperate to break free. Her hands were locked tight; she imagined she could see a heartbeat pulsing between the knuckles.

And yet, when she muttered under her breath that she would not let herself be pushed off course, no, not by anything, it wasn't the side-winds she was thinking of, but Amlis Vess. He was blowing in from somewhere much more dangerous than the North Sea, and she could not predict the effect he'd have. Whatever it turned out to be, she certainly wouldn't be able to negate it just by keeping a tight grip on her car's steering wheel.

She was past the mid-point now, minutes away from the Inverness end. Burring slowly forwards in the outer lane, she flinched every time a faster vehicle roared past her; the wind pressure would drop away suddenly, then swing back with a vengeance. To her left, the air was swirling with seagulls, a chaos of white birds endlessly falling towards the water, then hovering just above the firth, sinking gradually, as if caught in sediment. Isserley returned her attention to the distant outskirts of Inverness, and tried to force herself to tread harder on the accelerator. Judging by her speedometer, she wasn't succeeding. *You-ou-ou-ou-ou-ou!* cried the wind all the rest of the way.

Cruising safely off the bridge at the far end, she hugged the slow lane, tried her best to breathe deeply and unclench her hands. The pressure had died down almost at once; she could drive normally, function normally. She was on terra firma now, in control, blending in perfectly, and doing a job only she could do.

Nothing Amlis Vess thought or said could change that: nothing. She was indispensable.

The word troubled her, though. *Indispensable*. It was a word people tended to resort to when dispensability was in the air.

She tried to imagine herself being dispensed with; tried to imagine it honestly and unflinchingly. Perhaps some other person would be prepared to make the same sacrifices she and Esswis had made, and take her place. She and Esswis had been desperate, in their different ways; might not other people be equally desperate? It was hard to imagine. No-one could be as desperate as she had been. And then, anyone new to the job would be inexperienced, untested. With mind-boggling amounts of money at stake, would Vess Incorporated take such a risk?

Probably not. But it was difficult for Isserley to draw much comfort from this, because the thought of being genuinely indispensable was troubling too.

It meant that Vess Incorporated would never let her go.

It meant that she would have to do this job forever. It meant that a day would never come when she could enjoy the world without worrying about the creatures crawling on its surface.

All of which, Isserley reminded herself irritably, should have nothing whatsoever to do with Amlis Vess. How could it? Whatever the reason for young Amlis's visit, it must be a purely personal one, unconnected to Vess Incorporated. Just hearing the name Amlis Vess was no reason to get all excited.

OK, granted, Amlis was the big man's son, but there

was no sign of him inheriting the big man's empire. Amlis didn't even have a *job* at Vess Incorporated – he'd never had a job of *any* kind – and he couldn't possibly have any power to make decisions on the Corporation's behalf. In fact, to the best of Isserley's knowledge, Amlis actually felt disdain for the world of business and was a big failure in his father's eyes. He was trouble, but not for Isserley. There was nothing to fear from him dropping in, however inexplicably, on Ablach Farm.

So why did she want to avoid him so badly?

She had nothing against the boy himself (or the man? – how old would he be by now?); he hadn't asked to be the sole heir of the world's biggest corporation. He'd done nothing to offend her personally, and in the past she'd followed his exploits with amusement. He was always in the news, for the usual rich-young-pretender reasons. One time, he shaved all his hair off, as an initiation rite into a bizarre religious sect which he joined in a blitz of publicity and left, weeks later, with no comment to the press. Another time, he and his father were reported to be bitterly estranged over Amlis's support of extremists in the Middle East. Another time, he made a public statement that icpathua, when used in small enough doses, was a harmless euphoric that should not be against the law. Countless times, some girl or other made a fuss, claiming to be pregnant with his baby.

All in all, he was just another typical rich kid with a colossal fortune hanging over his head.

Isserley's second nature, alert while she'd been busy brooding, fetched her back into the driver's seat to notice something important: a hitch-hiker standing in the distance, opposite the first of the many garish roadside diners between Inverness and the South. She listened to her own breathing, assessing whether she'd calmed down enough to take the challenge on. She felt she had.

At closer quarters, though, the figure at the roadside proved to be a female, harried-looking, grey-haired, shabbily dressed. Isserley drove straight past, ignoring the appeal to shared gender in the eyes. A single instant was enough to communicate injury and dejection, then the figure was a dwindling fleck in the rear-view mirror.

Isserley was all geared up now, grateful to have had her mind on something other than Amlis Vess. Fortuitously, another hitcher was standing only a couple of miles further on. This one was a male, and fairly impressive on first sight, but unfortunately positioned in a spot where only the most foolhardy motorist would consider stopping. Isserley flashed her headlights, hoping to let him know that she might have picked him up had he not made it so dangerous for her to do so. She doubted that a simple flash of lights could communicate this; more likely he would simply assume she was beaming out ill-will, a jab of mockery.

All was not necessarily lost, though – perhaps she would see him again later on the way back, by which time he might have walked to a safer spot. Over the years, Isserley had learned that life often offered a second chance: she had even picked up hitchers who, many hours and miles before, she'd observed climbing gratefully into someone else's car.

So, optimistic, Isserley drove on.

She drove all day, backwards and forwards between Inverness and Dunkeld, over and over. The sun set. The snow, which had retreated during the morning, returned. One of the windscreen wipers developed an annoying squeal. Fuel had to be bought. Through it all, nobody suitable reached out to her.

By six o'clock, she had just about decided why she was dreading meeting Amlis Vess so much.

It had nothing to do with his status really; *she* was an invaluable part of the business, *he* a thorn in its side, so he probably had more to fear from Vess Incorporated than she did. No, the main reason why she was dreading him was simpler than that.

It was because Amlis Vess was from home.

When he set eyes on her, he would see her the way any normal person from home would see her, and he would be shocked, and she would helplessly have to watch him being shocked. She knew from experience what this felt like; would do anything to avoid feeling it again. The men she worked with on the farm had been shocked too, at first, but they were used to her now, more or less; they could go about their business without gawping (though if there was a lull in activities she always felt their eyes on her). No wonder she tended to keep to her cottage – and why Esswis did too, she guessed. Being a freak was so wearying.

Amlis Vess, never having seen her before, would recoil. He'd be expecting to see a human being, and he would see a hideous animal instead. It was that moment of . . . of the sickening opposite of recognition that she just couldn't cope with.

She decided to return to the farm immediately, lock herself in her cottage, and wait until Amlis Vess had come and gone.

In the mountainous desolation of Aviemore she caught a hitcher in her headlights. A little gargoyle gesturing in a flare of illumination, registering almost as an after-image on the retina; a little gargoyle foolishly attached to a spot where cars would be whizzing by him at maximum speed. Isserley's maximum speed being about fifty, however, she had time to notice him. He seemed awfully keen to be picked up.

Passing him, Isserley thought seriously about whether she wanted a hitcher just now. She waited for clues from the universe.

The snow had died down again, the windscreen wipers lay still, the motor was purring nicely, she was perhaps in slight danger of dozing off. Isserley slowed, cruised to a stop in a bus bay, and let the car idle, headlights dimmed. The Monadhliath Mountains loomed on one side of her, the Cairngorms on the other. She was alone with them. She closed her eyes, slid her fingertips under the rims of her glasses and rubbed her big satiny eyelids. A massive tanker roared into view, flooding the cabin of Isserley's car with light. She waited until it had gone, then revved her engine and flicked on the indicator.

On the second approach, passing by on the other side of the road, she noted that the hitcher was small and barrel-chested, with lots of exposed flesh so darkly tanned it resisted being bleached by the full beam of headlights. This time she observed that he was standing not far from a car which was parked, or possibly stuck, in a ditch off the road. It was a shabby blue Nissan estate, scratched and battered all over but not in such a conspicuously fresh way as to suggest an accident. Both hitcher and car seemed upright and in one piece, although the one was making exaggerated gestures to draw attention to the other.

Isserley drove on for a couple of miles, reluctant to involve herself in anything that might already be of interest to the police or a vehicle rescue service. Eventually, however, she reasoned that if a stranded motorist had any expectation of being found by such authorities, he surely wouldn't be trying to hitch. She turned around then, and drove back.

The final approach revealed the hitcher to be an odd creature, even by Scottish standards. Though not much taller than Isserley, with a wizened, wispy-haired little head and spindly legs, he had improbably massive arms, shoulders and torso, as if these had been transplanted onto him from a much beefier creature. He was wearing a frayed and faded flannelette shirt, sleeves rolled up, and seemed impervious to the cold, thumbing the bitter air with almost clownish enthusiasm, making elaborate gestures towards his decrepit Nissan. Isserley wondered momentarily whether she had seen him somewhere before, then realized she was confusing him with certain cartoon characters on early-morning television. His kind weren't the title characters, though; they were the ones who got squashed flat by giant mallets or burnt to a crisp by exploding cigars.

She decided to stop for him. He had more muscle mass packed in between his neck and hips, after all, than many vodsels twice his size had on their entire bodies.

Seeing her slow down and veer towards him, he nodded idiotically and held two stiff-thumbed fists aloft in an expression of triumph, as if awarding her two points for her decision. Above the crunch of gravel, Isserley thought she could hear a throaty whoop.

She parked as close as she could to the stranger's own car without snaring her wheels in the ditch, and trusted that her flashing rear lights would warn any motorists coming up behind her. This really was a very awkward spot, and she was curious to find out if the hitcher would acknowledge it. That would already tell her something worth knowing about him.

She wound down the passenger window as soon as she'd pulled on the handbrake, and the hitcher immediately poked his tiny head into the car. He was smiling broadly, a mouthful of crooked brown-edged teeth inside two leathery crescents of lip. His brown face was bristly, wrinkled and scarred, with a mottled snout of a nose and two spectacularly bloodshot chimpanzee eyes.

'She's gonna skelp my bot, I tell ya,' he leered, breathing alcohol into the car.

'I beg your pardon?'

'My girlfriend. She's gonna skelp my bot,' he repeated, his grin deepening to a grimace. 'I shoulda been at her place by tea-time. That's *always* when I'm supposed to be there. And it *never* happens, can you believe it, eh?' He slumped a little in the window-frame and his eyes closed slowly, as if the power that was keeping his eyelids up had abruptly run out. With effort he roused himself, and continued, 'Every week this same thing.'

'What same thing?' asked Isserley, trying not to pull a face at the beer fumes.

He winked, laboriously. 'She's got a temper.' Eyes falling shut again, he sniggered, like a cartoon tomcat in the shadow of a falling bomb.

Isserley found him actually quite good-looking compared to other vodsels, but his mannerisms were distinctly odd and made her wonder if he was mentally defective. Would an imbecile be given a licence to drive? Why was he just hanging in her window-frame, simpering, when both their cars were liable to get annihilated by a passing lorry? Nervously she glanced in her rear-view mirror to confirm no speeding vehicles were coming up behind.

'What happened to your car?' she asked, hoping to shift his attention to the heart of the matter.

'It won't go no more,' he explained dolefully, his eyes crusty slits. 'No more. That's the truth. No use arguin', eh? Eh?'

He grinned fiercely, as if hoping to charm her into dropping some opposing point of view.

'Engine trouble?' prompted Isserley.

'Nah. I ran out of petrol, like,' he said, snorting with embarrassment. 'On account of my girlfriend, y'understand. Every minute counts, with her. But I shoulda put in more petrol, seemin'ly.'

He squinted into Isserley's giant eyes, and she could tell he saw nothing more exotic there than the imagined reproach of a fellow motorist.

'The fuel gauge is a piece a'shite, you see,' he elaborated, stepping back from Isserley's car to display his own. 'Says empty when it's near full. Says full when it's near empty. Can't listen to a word it tells ya. Ya just have to rely on your memory, y'understand?' He yanked the door of his car open, as if intending to give Isserley a guided tour of its frailties. The light went on in the cabin – a pale and flickering light, attesting to the vehicle's dodgy reputation. Beer cans and crisps packets littered the passenger seats.

'I been up since five this morning,' the snout-nosed hitcher declared, banging his car's door shut. 'Worked ten days straight. Four – five hours sleep a night. Wicked. Wicked. No use complainin', though, eh? Eh?'

'Well … can I give you a lift, perhaps?' suggested Isserley, waving her thin arm in the empty space over her passenger seat, to capture and hold his attention.

'It's a can of petrol I'm needin',' he said, lurching into the window-frame of Isserley's car again.

'I haven't got any,' said Isserley, 'But get into the car anyway. I'll drive you to a garage, or maybe further. Where were you heading?'

'To my girlfriend's place,' he leered, winching his eyelids up off his eyeballs again. 'She's got a temper. She'll skelp my bot.'

'Yes, but where is that exactly?'

'Edderton,' he said.

'Get in, then,' she urged. Edderton was only five miles out of Tain, thirteen miles or so from Ablach Farm. How could she lose? If she had to give him up, she could soothe her disappointment by retreating instantly to the farm; if she took him, so much the better. Either way she'd be safe in her cottage by the time Amlis Vess arrived, and might even sleep through all the brouhaha – as long as nobody came knocking on her door.

Hitcher safely strapped in, Isserley pulled away from the gutter and accelerated up the A9 towards home. She regretted that this stretch of the road was unlit and that she couldn't legally turn on the cabin light; she would have liked this guy to have the opportunity to examine her properly. She sensed he was dim-witted, and likely just now to be fixated on solving his immediate problems; he might well need extra enticement to talk about himself. The darkness of the road, however, made her too nervous to drive with only her right hand on the steering wheel; he would just have to strain his eyes a bit, that's all, if he wanted to see her breasts. Admittedly, his eyes looked pretty strained already. She faced front, drove carefully, and left him to it.

She would throw him out on his arse, for sure, the hitcher was thinking, but maybe she'd let him sleep a bitty first.

Ha! No chance! She'd make him look at an oven dish full of dried-out supper, and say it couldn't be et now even though he'd be desperate to get stuck into it, but she wouldn't let him of course. That's what he drove like a maniac up the A9 for, every week, week after week. His girl. His Catriona. He could lift her up and toss her through the window like a vase if he wanted to, and *she* was the one who pushed *him* around. What was that all about, eh? Eh?

This girl who'd picked him up, now. *She'd* probably be all right. As a girlfriend, like. She'd let him sleep when he was dying for it, he could tell. She wouldn't poke him just when he was drifting off and say, 'You're not falling asleep are you?' Kind eyes, she had. Bloody big knockers, too. Pity she didn't have any big containers of petrol tucked away somewhere. Still, he couldn't complain, could he? No use complaining. Face the future with a smile, as the old man always used to say. Mind you, the old man never met Catriona.

Where was this girl going to drive him? Would she be willing to drive him back to his car again if he could get some petrol? He hated to leave his car in a ditch like that. A thief could steal it. Thief'd need petrol, though. But there were probably car thieves driving all around the countryside, with big petrol containers in the boot, just looking for a car like his. How low could some people go, eh? Dog eat dog, that's what it all boiled down to.

Catriona would murder him if he turned up any later than he already was. That wasn't so bad in itself, but she wouldn't let him sleep, this was the thing. If he could get some petrol into his car he could sleep in that, and maybe visit Catriona in the morning. Or sleep in the car all weekend even, sit around in Little Chefs during the day and drive back down to work on Monday morning.

Fucking great, eh? Eh?

This girl here wouldn't mind if he rested his head back on the seat for just a few minutes, would she? He wasn't much of a talker anyway. 'Thick as two planks,' Catriona always said.

But how thick exactly was a plank, eh? It just depended on the plank, didn't it, eh?

Isserley coughed, to summon him back to consciousness. Coughing didn't come easily to her, but she tried every so often, just to see if she could pull it off convincingly.

'Eh? Eh?' he yapped, his bloodshot eyes and snot-shiny snout leaping out of the dimness like startled wildlife.

'What do you work at?' said Isserley. She'd been quiet for a minute, assuming the hitcher was ogling her, but a strangled snort from his direction had let her know he was falling asleep.

'Woodcutting,' he said. 'Timber. Eighteen years in the business, eighteen years behind a chainsaw. Still got two arms and two legs! Heh! Heh! Heh! Not bad, eh? Eh?'

He held his fingers up above the dashboard and wiggled them, presumably to demonstrate that he had all ten.

'That's a lot of experience,' complimented Isserley. 'You must be well known to all the timber companies.'

'Yeah.' He nodded emphatically, his chin almost bouncing off his barrel chest each time. 'They run when they see me coming. Heh! Heh! Heh! Ya got to keep smiling, eh?'

'You mean, they're not satisfied with your work?'

'They say I'm not a good time-keeper,' he slurred. 'I

keep the trees waiting too long, y'understand? Late, late, late, that's me. La-a-a-a-ate ...' His head was slumping, the attenuated vowel describing a slow lapse into oblivion.

'That's very unfair,' Isserley remarked loudly. 'It's how well you do your job that matters, not the hours you keep, surely.'

'Kind words, kind words,' simpered the woodcutter, staring ever deeper into his lap, his tufty hair slowly rearranging itself on his compact skull.

'So,' exclaimed Isserley, 'you live in Edderton, do you?'

Again he snorted to the surface.

'Eh? Edderton? My girlfriend lives there. She's gonna skelp my bot.'

'So where do *you* live?'

'Sleep in the car through the week, or bed and breakfast. Work ten days straight, thirteen sometimes. Start five in the morning summertime, seven in winter. Or I'm suppo-o-o-o-sed to ...'

She was just about to rouse him from his slump when he roused himself, shifted around in his seat and actually laid his cheek against the headrest, pillow-style. He winked again, and, with a weary obsequious smile, mumbled across to her,

'Five minutes. Just five minutes.'

Amused, Isserley drove in silence while he slept.

She was mildly surprised when, more or less exactly five minutes later, he jerked awake and stared at her dazedly. While she was thinking of something to say to him, however, he relaxed again, and laid his cheek back against the headrest.

'Nother five minutes,' he pouted placatingly. 'Five minutes.'

And once more he was gone.

Isserley drove on, this time keeping one eye on the digital clock on the dashboard. Sure enough, some three hundred seconds later, the woodcutter jerked awake again.

'Five minutes,' he groaned, turning his other cheek to the headrest.

This went on for twenty minutes. Isserley was in no hurry at first, but then a road sign alerted her to the fact that they would soon be driving past a services turn-off, and she felt she'd better get down to business.

'This girlfriend of yours,' she said, the next time he woke. 'She doesn't understand you, is that right?'

'She's got a temper,' he admitted, as if he'd been spurred to articulate this for the first time ever. 'She'll skelp my bot.'

'Have you ever thought of leaving her?'

He grinned so broadly it was like an incision slicing his head in two.

'A good girl is hard to find,' he chided her, barely moving his lips.

'Still, if she doesn't care for you ...' persisted Isserley 'For example, would she be worried about you if you didn't turn up tonight? Would she try to find you?'

He sighed, a long wheezy exhalation of infinite weariness.

'My money's good enough for her,' he said. 'And, plus, I got cancer in the lungs. Lung cancer, in other words. Can't feel it, but the doctors say it's there. I might not have long, y'understand? No use giving up a bird in the hand, y'understand? Eh?'

'Mmm,' replied Isserley vaguely. 'I see what you mean.'

Another sign reminding motorists that services were not far ahead flashed by, but the woodcutter was nuzzling into the seat again, mumbling, 'Five minutes. Just another five minutes.'

And again, he was gone, his boozy breath snortling gently.

Isserley glanced at him. He sat slumped, his head lolling against the headrest, his rubbery mouth open, his red-lidded eyes closed. He might as well have been pricked by the icpathua needles already.

Isserley thought about him as she drove through the soundproof night, weighing up his pros and cons.

On the pro side, the woodcutter's drunkenness and sleepless excesses were no doubt well understood by all who knew him; nothing would surprise them less than if he failed to turn up wherever he was supposed to be. The car would be found, full of empty alcohol containers, on a windswept ribbon of road through two mountain ranges; there would be no doubt that the driver had stumbled away, drunk, into a frozen expanse of bog and precipice. Police would dutifully search for the body, but be resigned from the outset that it might never be found.

On the con side, the woodcutter was not a healthy specimen: his lungs, by his own admission, were full of cancer. Isserley tried to visualize this; imagined someone slicing him open and being squirted in the face by a stream of malodorous black muck made of burnt cigarette tar and fermented phlegm. However, she suspected this was a lurid fantasy based on her own distaste at the thought of inhaling burning punk into her lungs. It probably bore no relation to what cancer really was.

She frowned, straining to recall her studies. She knew cancer had something to do with runaway cell reproduction... mutant growth. Did that mean that this vodsel had huge abnormal lungs crammed into his chest? She didn't want to cause any problems for the men back at the farm.

On the other hand, who cared if the lungs were too big? They could surely be discarded whatever size they were.

On the *other* hand, she felt squeamish about bringing a vodsel onto the farm which she knew to be diseased. Not that anyone had ever told her in so many words that it was wrong, but ... well, she had her own internal moral sense.

The woodcutter was murmuring in his sleep, a slack-lipped crooning sound like 'moosh'n, moosh'n, moosh'n', as if he were trying to placate an animal.

Isserley checked the clock on the dashboard. More than five minutes had elapsed; quite a bit more. She took a deep breath, settled back in her seat, and drove.

An hour or so later, she had bypassed Tain and was approaching the Dornoch Bridge roundabout. It struck her that the weather conditions were so different from what she had experienced earlier that day on the Kessock Bridge that they could have been on a different planet. Lit up against the pitch-black environs by strips of neon on long stalks, the roundabout glowed eerily in the windless, trafficless stillness. Isserley drove onto its steeply ascending spiral, glancing at the woodcutter to see if the blaze of light would wake him. He didn't stir.

Pootling gently along, high up off the ground,

Isserley's car described an arc on the surreal concrete labyrinth. So monstrously ugly was this structure that it could have been mistaken for something from inside the New Estates, were it not for the open sky above. Isserley veered to the left to avoid crossing Dornoch Firth, and started a steep descent into leafy gloom. Her headlights, on full beam, picked out the flank of the Jehovah's Witnesses' Kingdom Hall nestled below, then tunnelled into Tarlogie forest.

Remarkably, it was now that the woodcutter squirmed in his sleep; having failed to react to the merciless lights of the roundabout, he seemed to sense, despite the darkness, the forest pressing in on the narrow road.

'Moosh'n, moosh'n, moosh'n,' he crooned wearily.

Isserley leaned forward as she drove, peering into the almost subterranean blackness. She felt fine. The forest's underground effect was an illusion, after all, and so it could not exert the nauseous claustrophobic power of the New Estates. She knew the barrier keeping out the light overhead was nothing more than a feathery canopy of twigs, beyond which lay a comforting eternity of sky.

Minutes later, the car emerged from the forest into the pastured surrounds of Edderton. The dismal caravan salesyard welcomed her to this minuscule village. Street lights illuminated the defunct post office and the thatched bus shelter. There was no sign of life.

Isserley flipped the toggle for the indicator, even though there was no vehicle to see it, and brought the car to a stop in a spot where the light was brightest.

She nudged the woodcutter gently with her strong fingers.

'You're here,' she said.

He jerked violently awake, his eyes wild as if he was in immediate danger of being brained with a blunt instrument.

'Wha-wha-where?' he waffled.

'Edderton,' she said. 'Where you wanted to be.'

He blinked several times, struggling to believe her, then squinted through the windscreen and the passenger window.

'Zaddafact?' he marvelled, orienting himself in the oasis of familiar aridity outside. Clearly, he was having to concede that nowhere else could look quite like this.

'Gee, this is ... I dunno ...' he wheezed, grinning with embarrassment and anxiety and self-satisfaction. 'I must of fell asleep, eh?'

'I guess you must have,' said Isserley.

The woodcutter blinked again, then tensed up, peering nervously through the windscreen at the deserted street.

'I hope my girlfriend's not out,' he grimaced. 'I hope she don't see you.' He looked at Isserley, his brow wrinkling as he considered the possibility that this might offend her. 'What I mean to say is,' he added, even as he was fumbling to unclasp his seatbelt, 'she's got a temper. She's what-would-you-say ... jealous. Aye: jealous.'

Already out of the car, he hesitated to slam the door before he had found the right words to leave her with.

'And you're' – he drew a deep, rasping breath – '*beau*tiful,' he beamed.

Isserley smiled back, bone-weary all of a sudden.

'Bye for now,' she said.

* * *

about the **author**

Michel Faber

Michel Faber was born in the Netherlands and brought up in Australia. He now lives near Inverness, the area around which *Under the Skin* is set. In addition to the novel *Under the Skin*, which was shortlisted for the Whitbread First Novel Award and nominated for the Dublin Impac award, he has written a volume of short stories, *Some Rain Must Fall*, which won the Saltire First Book of the Year award, and two novellas, *The Hundred and Ninety-Nine Steps* and *The Courage Consort*. His second novel, *The Crimson Petal and the White* was published in 2002. His work has won numerous other prizes and has now been translated into many languages.

A short interview

How and why did you come to live in the north of Scotland?

My wife fell in love with Tarrel Farm (called Ablach in the book) in the same way that some people fall in love with a person. She knew she had to live there, so we saved up and emigrated to Scotland.

The novel touches on many themes and issues. What do you see as the central concern of the book?

All my books are about people trying to evolve out of an old, damaged self. Some characters find this easier than others. For Isserley it's terribly hard.

Did any particular events or experiences stimulate the choice of themes in *Under the Skin*?

I knew when I was writing the book that the farm would be sold soon and that we would have to leave. So in one sense *Under the Skin* was my farewell to Tarrel and my way of remembering vividly what it was like. Also, having landed in the north of Scotland where there was a lot of unemployment and rural decay and lousy food, I was thinking a lot about how British society treats its more vulnerable citizens. This led me to think of the vodsels.

Why did you feel the particular setting of Easter Ross and the A9 was appropriate?

I'd hitch-hiked along that road many times and knew it well. Easter Ross is a beautiful place and this contrasted effectively with the terrifying things that happen in the story. The beauty of nature reflects Isserley's desire to escape the ugliness of her predicament.

The sense of longing and unrequited love is very powerful in the novel, and the ending is tragic. Did you at any point consider the possibility of a conventional 'happy ending' to the story?

No. And I don't think the ending is tragic. Isserley

becomes part of nature and her suffering is over.

This novel seems quite typical of your work in focusing on a central female character. Can you explain why you select a woman's point of view?

Not really. A couple of my unpublished novels are filtered through the perspective of a male character but I do seem to prefer the female viewpoint. I grew up in Australia during the 1970s – quite a feminist environment – so that has something to do with it, I'm sure.

What authors have inspired you personally? Are there any fantasy novels which you particularly admire?

Kurt Vonnegut, Charles Dickens, Samuel Beckett, John Berger, lots of others. I'm also inspired by very bad books because they teach me what to avoid. My favourite fantasy novel is *Nine Princes in Amber* by Roger Zelazny.

Under the Skin **has now been translated into many languages. Why do you think it has had such a universal and wide appeal?**

I think it comes down to the quality of the writing. The prose makes vivid pictures materialise in your head, and the characters are carefully developed so that you really believe in them. The themes and plot of the book aren't particularly original. Lots of authors have written about these themes and the plot is kind of ridiculous when you examine it closely. It doesn't feel ridiculous while you're reading it because the writing makes everything so real.

discussion **points**

1. Characters

Isserley – To what extent does Isserley engage the sympathy of the reader? Do you sympathise with her more or less as the story progresses?

Amlis Vess – How far do you see Amlis as a conventional hero? To what extent is your response to him affected by his alien physical shape?

The hitch-hikers – Consider the hitch-hikers whom Isserley picks up. Rank them in order of how appealing they are as characters.

2. Themes

Responsibility – 'Nobody has any individual responsibility.'
Isserley says this ironically and reproachfully to Amlis when he protests that he personally had nothing to do with her rejection by the 'Elite' of their own country. However, when Amlis does take individual responsibility by releasing the 'vodsels', the result is a bloodbath. What message do you feel the book presents on the issue of personal responsibility?

Equality – 'We're all the same under the skin.'
The novel takes its title from this comment from
Amlis Vess. Consider some of the contradictions the
book throws up in the area of equality (class, race and
gender).

Humanity – In the book the aliens call themselves
'human' and the humans are 'vodsels'. Consider how
far Faber makes each group conform to conventional
ideas of 'humanity'.

Nature – Consider the role of nature in the book and
what it contributes to the reader's response. Think of
the landscape in which it is set. What might the
beauty of the sky, land and sea reflect in the story?

3. Summing up

Has the book altered your views at all to any of the
following: the unemployed/unattached; factory
farming; eating meat; the natural world; hitch-
hiking?

The ending – How far do you agree with the author
that Isserley's end is not tragic, since she returns to the
nature that she loves?

press **quotes**

'A fantastic first novel, in both senses… a moral fable about the lives of animals, human and otherwise, it eschews Aesopian simplicities in favor of a braided narrative, that, astonishingly, grows more complex as its moral becomes increasingly stark. A great first novel.'
– *Boston Book Review*

'Original and unsettling, Under the Skin is a deftly paced social satire, an Animal Farm for the new century.'
– *Wall Street Journal*

'… an awesome debut novel that displays immense talent. It is as if the essence of Iain Banks and John Fowles has been poured into one person, with added imagination and compulsion.'
– *Bookseller*

'The suspense and the shock tactics sit well next to fleshed-out characterisations. Already an award-winning short story writer, Faber's moody tales evoke talents such as Alan Warner and Anthony Burgess.'
– *The Times*

'Faber's writing is chaste, dryly humorous and resolutely moral. The fantastic is so nicely played against the day-to-day that one feels the strangeness of both … a remarkable novel.'
– *New York Times*

'Recalling writers such as Jim Crace and Russell Hoban, *Under the Skin*, like Faber's short stories, is an extremely assured and imaginative work. It'll get to you, one way or another. Of that there is no doubt.'
– *Observer*

'… profound and disturbing… Faber writes superbly … It is a far-reaching story about callousness, objectification and lack of empathy with other beings.'
– *Sunday Times*

'Alternately gorgeous and terrifying, lyrical and brutal, the book compels and teases: a growing need to turn the pages sneaks up on you quietly as Faber slowly reveals the various facets of his strange, elusive heroine.'
– *Newsday*

'… strange, adept, original … Would that more first novels were as adventurous or as funky and daring in their conception.'
– *Independent on Sunday*

similar **reads**

The Hundred and Ninety-Nine Steps by Michel Faber
(Canongate Books; ISBN: 1841953288)
While working at Whitby Abbey unearthing skeletons, archaeologist Sian finds relief from her nightmares and makes a decision about a relationship after solving an ancient mystery.

Morvern Callar by Alan Warner
(Vintage; ISBN: 0099449943)
Morvern becomes increasingly detached from reality following the suicide of her boyfriend. Having disposed of his body, she embarks on a series of wild and bizarre experiences.

The Bridge by Iain M. Banks
(Abacus; ISBN: 0349102155)
The story of a man in a coma is interwoven with a complex fantasy involving a surreal world set within the Forth Rail Bridge which seems to emanate from his unconscious mind.

The Midwich Cuckoos by John Wyndham
(Penguin Books; ISBN: 014118146X)
A group of strange and beautiful children who are born into an English village prove to be malevolent invaders from another planet who plan the destruction of all they encounter.

The Inheritors by William Golding
(Faber and Faber; ISBN: 0571192580)
A story told through the eyes of a community of gentle Neanderthals who are ousted from their territory by a new and more ruthless tribe – the ancestors of *homo sapiens*.

The Martian Chronicles by Ray Bradbury
(Voyager; ISBN: 0007119623)
A collection of short stories concerning the emigration of humans to Mars. After causing widespread destruction on Earth, the invaders show little respect for their new home.

competition

Your chance to win ten contemporary works of fiction signed by their authors.

The *Read Around Books* series was developed by Scottish Book Trust to encourage readers to widen their reading interests and discover writers they had never tried before. Has it been a success? We want to hear from you. Tell us if you have enjoyed this little series or not and if you did, do you have any suggestions for authors who should be included in the series in the future.

Writer to us now with the following information:

Name and address
Email address
Are you a member of a readers' group?
Name of reader's group

Send us the information above and we will enter you into our prize draw to be drawn on 22 August 2003.

Send to:
RAB Draw
Scottish Book Trust
137 Dundee Street
Edinburgh EH11 1BG

scottish **book trust**

What is Scottish Book Trust?

Scottish Book Trust exists to serve readers and writers in Scotland. We work to ensure that everyone has access to good books, and to related resources and opportunities.

We do this in a number of ways:

- By operating the Writers in Scotland Scheme, which funds over 1,400 visits a year by Scottish writers to a variety of institutions and groups
- By supporting Scottish writing through a programme of professional training opportunities for writers
- By publishing a wide variety of resources and leaflets to support readership
- By promoting initiatives such as National Poetry Day and World Book Day
- And through our Book Information Service, providing free advice and support to readers and writers, and the general public.

For more information please visit
www.scottishbooktrust.com

titles **in the series**

Available in the Read Around Books series

Iain Crichton Smith's *Murdo: The Life and Works,*
   by Douglas Gifford

Meaghan Delahunt's *In The Blue House,*
   by Gavin Wallace

Michel Faber's *Under the Skin,* by Mary Firth

Jonathan Falla's *Blue Poppies,* by Rosemary Goring

Janice Galloway's *Clara,* by David Robinson

Andrew Greig's *That Summer,* by Alan Taylor

Anne MacLeod's *The Dark Ship,* by Lindsey Fraser

Maggie O'Farrell's *After You'd Gone,* by Rosemary Goring

Suhayl Saadi's *The Burning Mirror,* by
   Catherine McInerney

Ali Smith's *Hotel World,* by Kathryn Ross

Muriel Spark's *The Comforters,* by Alan Taylor

Alexander Trocchi's *Young Adam,* by Gillian Mackay